MW00886375

Made in the USA
Monee, IL
28 March 2022

93675677R10072